TREETOPS (

Gulliver's Travels

WRITTEN BY JONATHAN SWIFT

Adapted by Sally Prue

Illustrated by Tony Ross

OXFORD
UNIVERSITY PRESS

OXFORD
UNIVERSITY PRESS

is a department of the University of Oxford.
It furthers the University's objective of excellence in research, scholarship,
and education by publishing worldwide in

Oxford   New York

Auckland   Cape Town   Dar es Salaam   Hong Kong   Karachi
Kuala Lumpur   Madrid   Melbourne   Mexico City   Nairobi
New Delhi   Shanghai   Taipei   Toronto

With offices in

Argentina   Austria   Brazil   Chile   Czech Republic   France   Greece
Guatemala   Hungary   Italy   Japan   Poland   Portugal   Singapore
South Korea   Switzerland   Thailand   Turkey   Ukraine   Vietnam

Oxford is a registered trade mark of Oxford University Press
in the UK and in certain other countries

Text © Sally Prue 2008

The moral rights of the author have been asserted

Database right Oxford University Press (maker)

First published 2008

British Library Cataloguing in Publication Data

Data available

ISBN: 978-0-19-911768-0

10 9 8 7 6 5 4

Cover illustration by Mike Spoor

Inside illustrations by Tony Ross

Printed in China by Imago

Paper used in the production of this book is a natural, recyclable product
made from wood grown in sustainable forests. The manufacturing process
conforms to the environmental regulations of the country of origin.

Contents

PART 1

CHAPTER I

Shipwrecked

I had always dreamed of going to sea, and so it was with great excitement that I set sail on the ship *Antelope* on 4th May 1699. I was hoping for great adventures – but my travels took me to lands stranger and more dangerous than anything I had ever imagined.

The *Antelope* took me halfway round the world, but when we were north-west of Tasmania* we met a great storm that blew us onto a rock and split the poor *Antelope* into pieces. A few of us managed to get away in a rowing boat, but after about half an hour a huge gust of wind capsized* it and threw us into the sea.

I don't know what happened to the others, but I was carried along on enormous waves for a long time before I saw land. By the time I'd managed to fight my way ashore, I was so exhausted that all I could do was throw myself down and sleep.

I must have slept all night, because when I woke up the sun was high in the sky above me. I tried to turn over – and that was when I found to my horror that my arms and legs and even my hair were tied to the ground with hundreds of pieces of string.

As if that wasn't bad enough, I realised that something was crawling up my leg.

I squinted down hastily and saw the last thing I was expecting.

It was a little man. He was about half as long as my foot, and he was holding a bow and arrow.

I screamed with shock and struggled to get free. The little man ran off as fast as his legs would carry him, but at once a flight of tiny arrows stabbed into my face with a sting like a hundred needles. I fell back, groaning with pain.

All I could do was to keep still and hope the little people would stop shooting.

I soon felt the little man climbing back up on top of me. He made a speech – in a language I couldn't understand – and then a whole procession of little people climbed up and fed me bullet-sized loaves and joints of meat from an animal about as big as a mouse. They also gave me a tiny barrel of wine to drink.

I soon fell asleep again (because, as I found out later, the wine contained a sleeping potion) and the next time I woke up I discovered they had moved me. I was now chained by the leg to the wall of a grand building that was nearly as tall as I was.

There must have been a hundred thousand little people standing round gawping at me, and all I could think of to do was to sit and gawp back.

One spiteful man tried firing another arrow at me, but a man in a gold helmet ordered him to be tied up and prodded forward so I could reach him. I picked him up and pretended I was going to bite his head off – which made him screech and struggle like anything – but instead I cut his ropes with my penknife and let him go.

It was very lucky indeed that I let him go, because that made the man in the gold helmet, who was the king, decide I wasn't dangerous after all. So, instead of killing me, he ordered his people to bring me food and bedding.

But I was still left chained to the wall.

CHAPTER 2

The land of Lilliput

Over the next few days I was as gentle as possible with the people of Lilliput – that was the name of the island – because that seemed my best chance of them setting me free. I began to learn their language, too. The children soon got up courage to play hide-and-seek in my hair, and the young people even held a dance on my head.

Every day I asked the king to undo my chains, and in the end he agreed. Before I was set free, though, the king's admiral,* Skyresh, made me promise not to tread on people, and to be helpful to the king. In return, the king promised to give me enough food for 1,728 of his people.

I was twelve times taller, wider and *deeper* than a Lilliputian, so this was exactly fair.*

Once I was free I began to explore Lilliput. It was an extraordinary place, and the people carried on in some very odd ways. The children, for instance, lived in nurseries and only saw their parents twice a year. The boys were taught to do the same jobs as their fathers, and the girls learned housework, though the girls also learned to read, so they would be good company for their husbands.

The people of Lilliput seemed to find that these arrangements for the children worked all right, but I'm afraid all was not well in other ways.

It was partly the king's fault. He loved being the tallest, and so he gave all the best jobs at Court to people who wore low-heeled shoes. This, of course, annoyed all the people who liked wearing *high* ones. His son, the prince, did his best to stop people quarrelling by wearing one high heel and one low one, but this just made him fall over a lot, and everybody laughed at him.

As if this wasn't bad enough, the little people of the next-door island of Blefuscu were threatening to invade. Lilliput and Blefuscu had been at war for years because the Blefuscans insisted on doing something that the Lilliputians thought was very wicked. I didn't really understand it myself, but whenever a Blefuscan ate a boiled egg, he always opened it at the Big End. The Lilliputians always opened *their* boiled eggs at the Little Ends. Everyone in Lilliput seemed to think this was very important.

The Lilliputians were extremely worried, because the Blefuscan warships were all ready to set sail.

I went to the king straight away and told him I would help defend Lilliput against the Blefuscans, even if it meant risking my life.

CHAPTER 3

—◆—

*War and treachery**

The island of Blefuscu lay about half a mile from Lilliput. I crawled through the sandy hills so I could have a good look at the Blefuscan warships without being seen. Then I went back and asked the king for some cables and some iron bars, which I bent into hooks.

It took me about half an hour to swim across the channel to the Blefuscan warships. Luckily, the Blefuscans were so terrified at the sight of me that they all jumped overboard and swam away to shore.

I had to work fast because the Blefuscans started firing thousands of arrows. They hurt like anything, and if I hadn't had glasses on,

I'd probably have been blinded.

As it was, I had more than a hundred arrows in my skin before all the warships were hooked onto my cables. Then I started swimming back to Lilliput, towing them behind me.

There were crowds of Lilliputians waiting anxiously on the beach. At first they were terrified because they thought the Blefuscans were invading, but I put my head up out of the water and shouted, *'Long Live the King of Lilliput!'*

And then everyone cheered, and the king made me a *nardac,** which is the same as a duke.

I was very pleased to have saved Lilliput, and when the king came to see me I thought he'd come to say thank you. Far from it. He wanted me to go back and steal all the Blefuscans' boats so he could make himself king of Blefuscu. And then, of course, he could make them open all their eggs at the Small Ends.

Well, saving Lilliput was one thing, but making the Blefuscans do something they thought was wicked was quite unfair. So I told the king I wouldn't do it. He was very angry, and, looking back, I think that was when he began to wonder if I was more trouble than I was worth.

Not long after that, though, I was able to help the king with something very important. One night I was woken up by shouts of *Burglum!*, which means *Fire!*

I hurried towards the noise as fast as I could (luckily there was a moon, so I could see well enough not to tread on people) and found the queen's rooms in the palace ablaze. People were running about with buckets of water, but these were so tiny that they weren't doing much good. I'm sure the whole palace would have burned down if I hadn't had an idea.

There was an iron tank nearby into which all the palace sewers emptied. It was a bit smelly but I snapped off the pipes leading into it, heaved it up, and threw the contents on the flames.

In this way I was able to put out the whole fire in three minutes, and save the palace.

I *think* the king was grateful. The queen, however, was furious at the way I'd done it, and refused to live in her rooms ever again.

I met some Blefuscans soon after that. They were very friendly, especially after I explained that I didn't want any more wars. They invited me to visit their country, and I began looking forward very much to going.

But then a friend came secretly to see me with terrible news.

Admiral Skyresh was jealous that I'd defeated the Blefuscan fleet without him and he had accused me of planning to fight for the Blefuscans. Skyresh wanted me killed – and the queen and most of the king's council* agreed with him. I would be put on trial, and when I'd been found guilty they'd put powder on my clothes that would make me tear myself to pieces.

The council had almost agreed to this when someone suggested I should be blinded instead of killed, so I could still do useful work for the country.

In the end they decided I should be blinded and then starved to death. That way, by the time I died, I'd be thin enough to cut up easily – though they thought they'd keep my skeleton as a souvenir.

I felt very angry and sad when I heard all this. In some ways, I wanted to stay and explain everything at my trial, but I knew I was certain to be found guilty whatever I said.

I was so angry that it was only my promise not to harm the Lilliputians that stopped me knocking the whole country to pieces.

I went to the harbour, borrowed a warship to carry my things, and swam over to Blefuscu.

A few days after I reached Blefuscu, I was walking along the north-east coast when I spotted a capsized boat in the sea. It looked big enough to carry me. I got it back to shore with the help of several ships and about three thousand sailors.

The king of Blefuscu wanted me to stay with him for ever. But I'd had enough of kings, so I told him I'd rather go away than cause any more trouble between Blefuscu and Lilliput.

I patched up the boat I'd found, greased it* with the fat from three hundred cattle and made a sail out of thirteen thicknesses of linen.* I took some live cattle, and sheep too, to breed when I got home. Some of the little people wanted to come with me, but the king strictly forbade it.

I left Blefuscu on 24th September 1701 and three days later I saw a big sail.

The captain of that ship was Mr Biddle, and when I told him my story he thought I was quite mad until I got my sheep and cattle out of my pocket.

I reached home on 13th April 1702. I made quite a lot of money showing people my little animals, but I was still eager to see the world. I had no idea then that my next voyage was going to take me to a place even more extraordinary and dangerous than Lilliput. So I sold my animals and got a job on board the ship *Adventure*.

PART 2

CHAPTER 4

A giant adventure

The *Adventure* set sail on 20th June 1702 and we had reached the Straits of Madagascar* when violent gales blew us so far off course we lost all sense of where we were.

We got very short of fresh water, but on 15th June 1703 the boy on the topmast at last sighted land, and I rowed ashore with a group of armed men.

There was neither sight nor sound of a river, so we spread out to search for water. I'd walked about a mile when I looked out to sea and to my great horror I saw my friends rowing away as if their lives depended on it. And perhaps it did, for a moment later a great giant appeared, wading out after the boat.

I didn't wait to see what would happen. I ran away until I came to a path. I soon found myself jogging through a field of grass that was taller than I was, and then into another field of towering golden corn.

Things were not looking good, and they soon got worse. There was a noise like thunder, and eight huge giants appeared, each striding towards me swinging a scythe* with a blade big enough to slice through an oak tree.

I forced my way into the corn, out of sight, but the stalks were like young trees and I could hardly get between them. The giants were working towards me, cutting the corn, and I had nowhere to hide.

I stayed as still as I could, though I was expecting to be seen, grabbed and eaten with every passing moment. But then one of the giants' feet came down so near me that I couldn't help letting out a scream of terror. The creature heard that. It looked up, round, and down, and then it spotted me.

It looked at me carefully, as if to make sure

I wouldn't sting. Then it picked me up between finger and thumb. It squeezed me so I could hardly breathe, but I didn't dare struggle because it'd lifted me up higher than a roof top and I was terrified it would drop me.

I don't know what the creature made of me, but it took me to show his master, the farmer. The farmer blew my hair up to look at my face and then put me back down on the ground on all fours.

There was no chance of escaping, so I thought I'd better be polite. I stood up and bowed.

Well, the farmer carried me home wrapped in his handkerchief and showed me to his wife. She screamed, but once she realised I wasn't a sort of giant spider she was very kind. She minced me some meat, and the whole family, which included a girl and a baby, sat round to watch me eat. They were quite amazed when I took out my knife and fork.

There was a fierce-eyed cat in the house, as well as two dogs, each the size of about four elephants. All the animals were wary of me, but the baby grabbed me and would have bitten me in two if I hadn't screamed and made it drop me. Luckily, the farmer's wife just managed to catch me in her apron, or the fall would probably have killed me.

After dinner the wife put me on her bed and gave me a scarf as a cover. I fell asleep exhausted, but a galloping noise soon woke me up. I opened my eyes to find myself on a bed the size of a tennis court with two wolf-sized rats charging towards me.

I just had time to jump to my feet and draw my sword before the first rat sprang at me. I managed to stab it, and the other one fled.

I was left panting and very shocked. If I'd taken off my sword-belt before I went to sleep then I'd certainly have been torn to pieces.

The rat wasn't quite dead, so I killed it with another slash of my sword. It was a huge beast, with a tail very nearly as long as I was.

The farmer's wife was horrified when she found me all covered in blood, but I managed to make her understand that I was all right, but needed a bath. After I'd pointed to the door a few times, she even left me alone to have it.

The farmer's daughter was a very clever and kind girl. I called her Glumdalclitch, which means 'little nurse' in her language. She gave me her old doll's cradle to sleep in, and made me clothes out of stuff like sacking, which was the thinnest fabric she could find.

Glumdalclitch started teaching me to speak her language straight away, so that when all the neighbours came to see me I was able to say 'hello' to them.

My farmer soon realised he could make some money by showing me to people on market day. Glumdalclitch was terribly upset. She was afraid someone would pull my arms and legs off, but the farmer carried me to market anyway.

I was very grateful to Glumdalclitch. If she hadn't padded the box I travelled in, I might have been shaken to death on the journey. Being carried on the farmer's horse was worse than being in a ship in a high storm.

I had to perform to twelve sets of people that day, shouting answers to their questions and doing sword exercises. The farmer did take care of me, though. He wouldn't let anyone touch me, and when a boy threw a nut as big as a pumpkin at my head, the boy was given a severe telling off and told to leave the room. I made so much money for the farmer that he decided to show me all round the kingdom of Brobdingnag.

I set out with him and Glumdalclitch on 17th August 1703.

CHAPTER 5

The kingdom of Brobdingnag

I had to work so hard on my tour of the country that I got very thin, so when the queen saw me and wanted to buy me the farmer was delighted. He was expecting me to drop dead any minute.

I asked the queen to let Glumdalclitch stay with me, and of course Glumdalclitch was overjoyed to live in the palace.

The king was very interested in me too, and sent for three professors to make sure I wasn't clockwork.* The professors thought I was a baby until they looked through a magnifying glass and saw the stubble* on my chin, and after that they decided I was a sort of odd freak that had just popped up by mistake.

So the king, who was a sensible sort of person, sent the professors away. He had a fine box made for me to live in. And he often sent for me, so I could tell him about my travels. I must say, though, that he found it hard not to laugh at the idea that countries of such little creatures as me could think themselves important, and call themselves lords, or even kings.

This made me cross, but of course I was in no position to argue with him. In any case, I was getting used to the size of the enormous people around me. If I'd seen a group of humans strutting around thinking themselves very grand, I might well have laughed myself.

There was one person at court, though, who was jealous of my size. The queen had a very small page,* and before I arrived he'd been everyone's favourite. He decided to get rid of me. One day, when Glumdalclitch was at the other end of the room, he grabbed me and dropped me into a big bowl of cream.

It was lucky I was a good swimmer, for the queen was in too much of a panic to do

anything but screech. Even so, I had swallowed
a lot of cream before Glumdalclitch could
rescue me.

The page was beaten and made to drink all
the cream, but even so I felt a lot happier after
the queen sent him away to a friend. That place
was nerve-racking enough as it was, without
people trying to murder me. Even the *flies* were
dangerous in Brobdingnag, because some of
them were nearly as big as blackbirds. They'd
buzz around me while I was eating and could
bite really painfully. I spent half my mealtimes
slashing them away with my knife, which the
queen found hilarious.

Worse still, one day at breakfast there was a droning like twenty bagpipes and a swarm of wasps came in through the window. I leaped up and managed to kill four of them with my sword, but not before one of them carried off my piece of cake. The stings on the dead wasps were nearly as long as my little finger. I pulled them out and kept them carefully, and later gave them to a museum.

◆◆◆

I was surrounded by so many dangers in Brobdingnag that it wasn't often that Glumdalclitch left me alone. She was always worried about me. When she did leave me in peace, I enjoyed myself so much that I didn't

tell her about any adventures I had had.
Glumdalclitch never knew, for instance, about
the time a hawk swooped down on me and
I only just escaped by hiding under a thyme
bush. Or the time a frog jumped into the boat
the queen had had made for me and nearly
overturned it.

But there was no hiding my most terrible
adventure. I was sitting in my box one day when
there was a thumping on the wall and I saw two
bright eyes peering in through the open window.

My first reaction was to dive down into the
far corner of my box, but a great hand came in
and groped about. I did my best to avoid it, but
it caught me by the coat. Then it dragged me

out and I found myself cradled in the arms of the queen's pet monkey.

It didn't seem to want to hurt me, but it kept trying to shove disgusting bits of stuff into my mouth.

I was just beginning to wonder if I was going to survive this, when there was a noise at the door and the monkey jumped right out of the window and up onto the roof.

Everyone panicked. Glumdalclitch started screaming, the servants rushed to get ladders, and some of the people down below started throwing stones in the hope of frightening the monkey down.

Of course this panicked the monkey, too. He dumped me on the topmost ridge of the roof and bounced away. There I clung giddily, a quarter of a mile above the ground, expecting every moment to be blown to my death by the stiff breeze.

No one can know how grateful I was when a brave boy risked his life to climb up to me. I was half choked with the revolting stuff the monkey had tried to feed me, and I was so nearly squeezed to death that I had to go to bed for two weeks.

I spent a lot of time with the queen's ladies while I was recovering. They were great fun, but I have to say they *smelled* horrible. Mind you, I think this was partly because they were so big. Once when I was in Lilliput, a very good friend said the same about me after I'd been doing a lot of exercise.

But although everyone was very kind, people kept laughing at me. There was the time I tried to jump over a huge pile of mud and didn't find out it was dog's mess until I'd landed in the middle of it. That amused everyone hugely. The whole palace laughed for *days* about that.

CHAPTER 6

The wisdom of the king

I got so tired of being laughed at by everyone in Brobdingnag that I started making things, for I could do finer work with my small hands than any of the king's craftsmen. I made a purse out of the queen's hair, and even a comb from bits of the king's beard.

But it was when the king and I talked to each other that I was really able to show myself to be a clever and sensible man. As I pointed out to him, small creatures like bees are cleverer and more hard-working than many larger animals. After all, people don't always expect the tallest person to have the best brains.

The king was a wise man, and he wanted to

hear all about where I'd come from because he was hoping to find some good ideas he could copy in Brobdingnag.

So I told him all about everything. I told him about the army, our hobbies, the law, parliament,* and finished up with a quick trip through our history.

All this took several afternoons, and at the end of it all, the king, who had been taking notes, had a whole list of questions for me.

Now, Brobdingnag is completely cut off from the rest of the world, so the people there are very ignorant and backward. I think that was why the king hadn't really understood very much that I'd told him. His first question

was, how were our Members of Parliament* trained? And he was very surprised to find out they weren't actually trained at all.

I have to say, though, that the king didn't know very much about making up laws, because in Brobdingnag no law is allowed to be more than twenty-two words long. This means that even ordinary people can understand the laws perfectly well, so there is hardly any need for lawyers or politicians. I found this very strange indeed.

The king hadn't understood anything much I'd said about the army either. He couldn't understand why people meddled with things outside their own kingdom. He was also astonished by what I'd told him about our history, which seemed to him to be all murders, plots and rebellions.[*]

And when I told him about our marvellous invention, called a gun, that can shoot out bits of metal so hard it can sink ships holding a thousand men, or even knock the walls of cities down, he was filled with horror at the thought of so much blood and destruction. He said he'd rather lose half his kingdom than use such a thing, and he commanded me never to tell anybody else about it.

This was obviously very silly of him. But then, the king had such odd ideas that he thought that all you needed to run a country was common sense and fairness. This, of course, made him quite unlike any human ruler. He also said that anyone who could make two ears of corn grow where one had grown before would do more good for his country than any king.

When we got to hobbies, he was very puzzled by the idea of lotteries and gambling, and asked if it didn't make some people very poor and unhappy.

At last, when I'd explained everything as well as I could, the king closed his book of notes. And then he told me very gently that although I seemed a nice, honest sort of man, the little people who were the rulers of the countries I'd told him about seemed to be the nastiest collection of horrible creatures that ever crawled upon the face of the earth.

I was quite upset about him talking about humans like that. Perhaps the king found it hard to take us seriously because we were small.

After all, I'd felt much the same way about the leaders of Lilliput.

I always hoped that some day I'd go home from Brobdingnag. As I said, everyone was very kind – but I was longing to be able to walk about without being afraid of being trodden to death by a frog.

I'd been in Brobdingnag for about two years when the king and queen decided to visit their southern palace, which was near the coast. I journeyed quite comfortably in my travelling box. I even got a chance to enjoy the sun, which came through my skylight onto my hammock.

Poor Glumdalclitch, however, got a dreadful cold on the journey. She had to go to bed, and when a page took me down to the beach the sight of the waves that separated me from home made me so sad that I began to feel ill myself. I decided to have a lie down in my hammock while the page went off to look for birds' eggs.

I was woken up by my box jerking about so violently that it nearly tipped me out onto the floor. And before I knew what was happening, my box had shot up into the air and I was being carried away very fast.

I shouted for help but there was no answer, and when I heard a loud flapping above my head I realised my terrible danger. An eagle had picked up my box so it could smash it on the rocks. Then it could pick my body out of the wreckage and eat it, just as it did with tortoises.

There were a couple of huge bangs, and my box began to fall so fast I could hardly breathe.

The fall ended in a huge roaring noise and everything went dark. I'd given myself up for lost, when I began to rise up again and saw green light through my windows. My box was floating on the sea. I suppose my bird must have been attacked by other eagles, which made it drop me.

My box was leaking only a little, but my skylight was open and one big wave could easily tip my box over and sink it. Even if I didn't drown, I wasn't going to survive long at sea without water or food.

I spent about four hours lurching about on the water, expecting every moment to be my last, and in the end I heard a scratching sound and my box began to bob about in a different way, as if I was being towed.

I hurriedly unscrewed my chair from the floor and managed to fix it under my skylight. I climbed up on it and pushed up my stick with my handkerchief tied to the end of it, and screamed and bawled for help in all the languages I knew.

There was a yelp of surprise, and some

trampling over my head. Then my box bumped against something solid.

'Is anybody in there?' called a voice.

'Help!' I bellowed.

'We'll get a carpenter! We'll soon get you out!'

'No, no! Just lift my box out of the sea and then I can open the door!'

That caused a lot of laughter, and when someone had sawn a hole in the top of my box, I saw why.

I was so shocked to see people of my own size, I nearly fainted. But Mr Wilcocks, the captain, took me into his cabin and gave me a drink and let me have a rest on his bed.

I woke up feeling much better. Of course, everyone thought I was mad when I told them my story, especially as I shouted it all at the top of my voice. But I explained that talking to one of the people of Brobdingnag was like talking to a man on top of a cliff, and then I showed them my souvenirs from Brobdingnag, which included a footman's tooth and a corn* as big as an apple that I had cut off a maid's toe. Then they had to believe me.

Everything on the ship seemed so small to me that I had to be careful not to annoy the captain by laughing at it. The cups, for instance, looked no bigger than nutshells.

I had the same problem when I got back to England. Everything looked so tiny that I kept thinking I was in Lilliput again, and kept shouting at people to get out of my way. I was lucky to avoid getting into quite a few fights over that.

After a while, though, I stopped trying to pick people up, and I stopped crouching down whenever I needed to get through a doorway, and I stopped looking round for Glumdalclitch whenever I wanted something. I began to get used to life back in England.

But I didn't get to enjoy it for very long.

PART 3

CHAPTER 7

—◆◆◆—

The land of the eggheads *

I'd only been home ten days, when Captain
William Robinson of the ship *Hopewell* came
to see me. He was so eager for an experienced
sailor to join his ship that he offered me double
my usual wages. I really couldn't have refused to
sail then, even if I hadn't been full of curiosity to
see more of the world.

We set off on 5th August 1706 and bad luck
dogged us from the start. Lots of the crew got ill,
and we couldn't buy the goods we wanted. First,
we met bad weather and then, even worse,
pirates.

The pirates who captured the ship were going
to tie us back-to-back and throw us into the sea

to drown. But I pleaded with them to be merciful, and in the end they decided to keep the others to crew their ship. I'd annoyed the pirates so much with my begging and pleading, however, that they dumped me in a canoe and sailed away and left me.

Our position when the pirates attacked was 46 North, Longitude 183.*

I paddled away from the pirate ship feeling very anxious and lonely. There were several islands to the south-east, but when I reached them I found they were little more than rocks.

Luckily, it was the season for birds' eggs, which I cooked on a fire of dried seaweed. I made myself a bed of heathery stuff, and slept pretty well.

I spent the next few days exploring the islands, but by the fifth day I was close to despair. There were eggs to eat, but it was plain I couldn't survive on those islands for long.

I was wondering how long I had to live when a shadow fell over me. I looked round hastily and saw a great tower-shaped thing flying towards me across the sea. It must have been two miles high, and when it got nearer I could see there were people walking up and down steps on the side of it.

For a moment all I could do was stare, frozen with amazement. Then I started jumping up and down and shouting, and waving my handkerchief.

No one answered me, but several people began running up the stairs, and soon a long chain came down with a chair at the end, and I was lifted up to the floating island.

I'd thought that nothing could surprise me, but the men of that place, which was called Laputa, were really odd.

They wore long dresses covered with stars, and they had their necks bent over sideways so that one of their ears pointed straight up. Their eyes pointed upwards too. As if this wasn't peculiar enough, they had ordinary head-upright men with them, who kept hitting them with balloons.

I couldn't imagine why on earth they were doing this, but it turned out that the lopsided people were so clever that they never heard anything anyone said unless someone hit them on the ear to remind them to listen. In fact, the lopsided people were always so busy thinking that if it wasn't for the balloon-people they would always be walking into trees, or off the edge of the island. My lopsided guide was so clever that he forgot where he was going twice, just on the way up to the king's palace.

The lopsided king was too busy doing an experiment to notice me much, but I was treated quite kindly.

I was given a dinner of beef triangles (for the Laputans used science for everything) and then measured up for new clothes. This was done very cleverly with a compass and a lot of sums, but I'm afraid someone must have made a mistake somewhere because when the clothes arrived, one sleeve was much longer than the other.

Luckily, that sort of mistake seemed to happen a lot in that country, so I didn't feel too embarrassed. Their houses were nearly as lopsided as their clothes. The lopsided men were always too busy thinking to notice the draughts, but their wives got terribly fed up with them.

The flying island of Laputa was powered by a huge magnet and as it went along, the lopsided people let down strings so the people below could send them food. If the people below got fed up with having to give their food away, the king of Laputa would keep the island hovering over them so they got no sun or rain and all their crops died. The king could also drop rocks on their heads. If they *still* didn't give in, the king could drop the whole island on their heads.

The city of Lindalino did once defeat Laputa by putting another magnet in a tower and sticking the whole island there, but that was long ago.

CHAPTER 8

The College for Inventors

I soon got fed up with Laputa – the people were so clever I had no one to talk to. I waited until Laputa was hovering over a place called Lagardo, and then got myself set down on a chain in just the same way as I'd arrived.

It was a relief to be on firm ground again, but I found there was a terrible famine* in Lagardo. It turned out that their leaders had visited Laputa a few years before, and since then the people had been growing all their food by the latest scientific methods. In fact, they had set up a special College for Inventors, and they were sure that soon they'd be growing more food than they could eat.

Unfortunately none of these new methods was quite working yet, and so at the moment it was only in a few old-fashioned, unscientific areas that people had enough to eat.

Of course I was very curious to visit the College for Inventors, which had hundreds of rooms, and an inventor hard at work in each one.

In the first room I met a nice man whose clothes were rather burnt at the edges. He had a wonderful scheme for catching sunbeams in cucumbers and then letting them out again in cold weather. I had to lend him some money, though, because cucumbers were terribly expensive at that time of year.

There were so many inventors I can't describe
them all, but I can't leave out the man trying to
squash air into bricks, and the man who wanted
to build houses starting off with the roofs.

Oh, and there was someone else who had
made a machine that wrote truly original books
by putting words together in strange orders. This
man was very worried in case someone stole his
invention – but I promised him that although
people are always stealing new ideas, I was
certain no one would think of stealing this one.

There was one invention that would have worked very well, except that unfortunately the ladies and ordinary people refused to use it. It was an invention for saving people's breath. Instead of having to speak, you carried things about to show people. You could quite often see two clever men take off their backpacks and talk for ages by showing each other the things inside. Then they'd politely help each other on with their packs again and go on their way.

The college had a marvellous school, too, where the boys and girls learned things by eating slices of bread with their lessons printed on it. I'm afraid the children were very difficult, though. Not only did they keep on being sick, but they were always sneaking in ordinary food to eat, which stopped the invention working.

I suppose I should mention the law inventors at this point. They were mostly quite crazy, but they did have one good idea. Their plan was that whenever there was a problem, someone should stamp hard on a politician's feet every day until it was solved.

There were hundreds more inventors in the college, but I decided I'd be better off making my way home.

It turned out there was no boat sailing for Europe for a month, so I visited the island of Glubbdubdrib while I was waiting.

The people of Glubbdubdrib live very easy lives, because they have found a way to make the ghosts there look after them. The governor's palace was absolutely full of ghosts, and I'm sure they were very useful, but the sadness on the poor ghosts' faces made my flesh go cold with horror.

There were quite a few celebrity ghosts, so I grabbed the chance to speak to them. Aristotle, the oldest of them, was terribly grumpy, and said that Mr Newton's new theory of gravity would be out of date before we knew it. In fact, I'm afraid that nearly all the celebrities were a dreadful disappointment.

As one of them said to me, being nice is an awful nuisance if you're trying to get things done.

I left Glubbdubdrib to catch the ship for Luggnagg, and arrived there safely after being guided by pilots through the very dangerous sandbanks that guard the harbour.

When the king of Luggnagg heard about me he sent for me to come *and lick up the dust in front of him.*

Well, I thought this was just a saying, but when I got to court I found that anyone who visited the king really did have to crawl forward to his throne licking the floor as he went.

I was lucky, really, because they'd swept the floor, but sometimes if the king is annoyed with

someone he will have the floor covered in dirt
on purpose. If he is *very* annoyed with someone,
he will sprinkle down poison.

The strangest people I met in Luggnagg were
the *struldbergs*, who can live for ever. I was really
amazed when I first heard about them.

Why, I thought, if I could live for ever I'd
spend a couple of hundred years making my
fortune, and then I would learn everything
about everything and give everybody lots of
advice.

But when I visited a struldberg I changed my mind. It was horrible. The struldbergs never die, but they do get old. They lose their teeth, and their loved ones, and their memories, but they still live on and on, getting poorer and sicker for ever and ever.

The king of Luggnagg gave me a red diamond, which I later sold for a small fortune, but I left that country *very* gladly. I spent fifteen days on a voyage to Japan, and boarded the ship *Amboyna* there.

The *Amboyna* sailed with a fair wind, and on 16th April 1710, I landed in England after many years away.

PART 4

CHAPTER 9

The land of the Houyhnhnms

I had been at home for five months when I
was offered a job as captain of the *Adventure*.
I couldn't refuse such a huge honour. Besides, I
was beginning to long for adventures again, so I
set sail from Portsmouth on 7th September 1710.

I took on several new crewmen in Barbados,
but this was a terrible mistake. The men were
escaped pirates, and they hatched a plot to seize
my ship.

They held me prisoner in my cabin for several
weeks, but on 9th May 1711 they rowed me to a
beach and left me there.

I had no idea at all where I was, but I made
my way inland and soon came across a path

marked with the tracks of people and horses. I had some beads and rings in my pockets, and I decided that the only thing to do was to go and find the native people and use these trinkets to make friends.

I went along cautiously, keeping well hidden for fear of arrows, but saw nothing alive until I spotted some large animals up in a tree.

I was going to walk past, but one of the animals jumped down and bounded up to me. It had long hair on its head and sharp claws, and it was snarling viciously. I gave it a swipe with the flat of my sword to scare it off, but it bellowed so loudly that the whole group of creatures came to join it. All I could do was put my back against a tree and keep them off by waving my sword at them.

I was wondering how long I could keep this up when they all suddenly took fright and ran away as fast as they could.

I looked around to find out what had frightened them, but all I could see was a horse walking quietly along. The horse, which was a grey, threw up its head at the sight of me, but when I tried to walk past it, it kept getting in my way.

I tried making friends with it by patting its neck, but it didn't like this at all. It shook its head and nudged my hand away with its forefoot. Then it neighed three or four times in such an odd way that it almost sounded as if it was talking.

Another horse came along then, and the two horses touched forefeet and took it in turns to neigh to each other.

Well, I told myself that if the *horses* were this clever then the *humans* must be the wisest people on earth.

The two horses walked round me, inspecting me very carefully, neighing in a puzzled sort of way. I could only think they were really magicians who had turned themselves into horses for some reason.

'Gentlemen,' I said. 'I'm just a poor shipwrecked Englishman. Please show me the way to a village where someone can help me on my way.'

The horses listened to me, and began neighing seriously to each other again. I kept hearing them say the sound *yahoo*, so I said the word myself, imitating* their neighing speech.

The horses were very surprised at that. The grey repeated the word, as if it were trying to teach me a better accent, and then the other horse said another word – *houyhnhnm*. This took me several attempts, but I did well enough to amaze both the horses.

The grey said, *'Hhuun, Hhuun!'* and began to lead me along the road.

The grey led me to a long wooden building. I got my beads and rings ready to greet the master of the house, but inside the first room I found only horses. Two of them were sitting down like dogs, and another was sweeping the floor.

I was trying to decide whether this was all magic, or whether I'd just gone mad, when the grey led me into another room, and there, sitting on mats, were a very beautiful mare and a colt and a foal.

The mare looked at me down her nose and said, *'Yahoo,'* but the grey led us all out into a yard. Here, tied to a post, were three of the horrible creatures I'd seen earlier. They were busy feeding themselves by tearing some dead animal to pieces with their claws.

The grey untied the largest of the creatures, and he made us stand near each other so he could compare us. It was only then that I realised to my horror that the creature was really very like a human, except that he had longer nails and was quite a lot hairier.

It was lucky that I was wearing clothes, for this made me look more different from the creature, the Yahoo, than I actually was.

Not long afterwards four Yahoos pulled up
a sledge with a horse sitting on it, and all the
horses went in to dinner. They ate sitting on bales
of straw, and had oats first, followed by hay. The
horses talked a lot, and I spoke the words I knew,
and learned some more, though the horses'
language was very hard to pronounce.

After the meal I was hungry myself, so I said
one of the words I had learned, *hlunnh*, which
means oats. When I got some I rubbed all the
husks off, ground them between two stones, and
mixed them with water to make a sort of biscuit,
which I toasted in front of the fire. This, with
milk, was my main food all the time I lived in
that country, though sometimes I caught rabbits
with traps made of Yahoo hair. I also gathered

leaves for salads. I missed having salt, but I must say I kept quite healthy without it.

When it began to get dark the grey led me to a barn. I made myself a bed of straw, covered myself with my clothes and slept very well.

My master (for by now it was obvious that the grey was master of the whole household) was convinced I wasn't an ordinary Yahoo. This was partly because I was cleverer and cleaner than the other Yahoos, but mostly because he took my clothes to be my skin.

Well, I didn't want to be thought a Yahoo, and so I was careful not to let anyone see me without my clothes on. But then one day disaster struck. One of the horses, or Houyhnhnms, came out to my barn before I was awake and found me with my clothes fallen off beside me. He galloped away in a great fright, and after that of course I had to explain everything.

My master thought my clothes were clever, but now he knew that I looked exactly like a Yahoo, except for being balder and having shorter nails.

From that time I worked extra hard to learn the Houyhnhnms' language. I wanted to show my master just how different from the Yahoos I was. As soon as I had learned enough words, I told him I'd come across the sea on a ship, which I had to call a floating stable. My master shook his head at this, and said that I must have made a mistake, or that I was saying *the thing that was not* (the Houyhnhnms never tell lies, and so have no word for lying). My master had never heard of a Houyhnhnm making such a thing, so he was sure a Yahoo couldn't.

My master also found it hard to believe that in my country the Yahoos were the masters of the Houyhnhnms. He couldn't help wondering again if I was saying *the thing that was not,* which made him very uncomfortable. He was intelligent, but he could never get used to the idea that saying things that aren't strictly true is a normal part of human life.

It was hard to explain about the lives of horses at home. I started off with stables, food and grooming, but that just made him think that the horses were really in charge after all. So then I told him about saddles and carts – but he couldn't understand why the horses didn't roll over and squash any Yahoo that sat on its back.

So then, rather ashamed, I told him about spurs and whips.

My adventures filled my master with even greater astonishment. It took ages to explain what pirates were, and even then he couldn't understand why anyone would want to do such terrible things. My master reminded me of the king of Brobdingnag in that way.

'Hmm,' said my master thoughtfully. 'It's a good job your teeth and claws are too weak to hurt each other very much.'

So then I told him about guns and bullets and bombs, and told him that I had seen men blown up.

My master stopped me then, having heard enough of that. So I never got a chance to tell him about Admiral Skyresh in Lilliput.

CHAPTER 10

The final adventure

My master thought very carefully about everything I told him. In the end he decided that humans were really very much like Yahoos, because the Yahoos too, often fought each other over shiny stones or food, even when there was plenty of both.

I couldn't help but know that my master was right and that the Houyhnhnms lived much more peaceful lives than humans. The Houyhnhnms never had fights, and they were always just as kind to strangers as they were to their own families. Husbands and wives were chosen by the young ones' parents, and the Houyhnhnms always lived with these partners for the whole of their lives without either being in love, or quarrelling.

The young Houyhnhnms were strictly brought up to be clean, strong and hard-working. They were only ever allowed the plainest food. The females and males had the same education, which included lots of exercise, except that the females also learned about housework.

The Houyhnhnms lived peacefully and usefully until they were about seventy-five. When they realised they were going to die, they said goodbye to everyone quite quietly, and no one was at all sad.

The Houyhnhnms held a Council Meeting every four years to sort out any problems. One of these meetings took place when I was living with the Houyhnhnms, and I was proud to be able to make a suggestion to my master about the Yahoos. The Yahoos were really a dreadful nuisance to the Houyhnhnms. They killed the Houyhnhnms' cows, they trampled their oats, and they were dirty and nasty.

So I suggested to my master that they breed up donkeys to take their place.

And the Houyhnhnms thought that was a *very* sensible idea.

I was very happy with the Houyhnhnms, and I think that everything useful I know, I learned from them. The Houyhnhnms were wise and kind and strong, and the longer I lived with them the more I respected them and their ways.

I found myself avoiding looking at my reflection in streams, because I didn't want to see how much I looked like a Yahoo and, although I didn't realise it, I was beginning to move and speak like a horse. People make fun of me for it now, but I feel proud when they do.

But one terrible morning my master sent for me, and I saw by his face that he had something difficult to say. I had to leave the country. The

Council had decided that it wasn't sensible for my master to keep a Yahoo, because I was no use to Houyhnhnms. There was also a risk, the Council thought, of my organising the other Yahoos and leading them in a rebellion. The Yahoos were vicious and strong, and if they learned to use weapons they would be very dangerous. The Council said I must either be treated like the other Yahoos, or I must swim back to my own home.

I was filled with great sorrow. How could I go back to live in a place ruled by people who were so much like Yahoos?

My master and his friends helped me make a boat. It took six weeks to build.

My dear master came down to the shore to say goodbye. I said a respectful farewell, and then pushed my boat into the sea.

I left the Houyhnhnms. My plan was to find a small island where I could live alone, for the idea of living with Yahoos, even human ones, was quite revolting to me.

I steered eastward towards (I hoped) New Holland, and at dusk I spotted a very small island where I spent the night. In the morning I set sail again, and arrived in New Holland by nightfall.

I did not dare go far inland for fear of humans, but there were shellfish on the rocks that I could eat raw.

On the fourth day of living like this I was spotted by a herd of humans with bows and arrows.

I ran for my life and managed to push my boat out to sea, but one of the humans shot me in the knee before I had gone far. I was afraid the arrow was poisoned, so I sucked the wound as soon as I was out of range, and bandaged it as best I could.

I didn't dare land there again, so I sailed north, looking for a safe place. I saw a sail in the distance, but the thought of being with Yahoos or humans was so disgusting that instead I made for the shore and hid myself behind a rock.

But I was too late. The ship's lookout had spotted my boat, and the crew came and searched the shore until they found me.

None of the crew knew what to make of my Yahoo-skin coat, but one of them asked me who I was.

'I'm just a poor human,' I told them. 'Please let me go.'

They fell about laughing at that, because I spoke like a horse, but they told me their captain would take me to Lisbon, where I could get a ship home.

I begged them again and again to let me go – but they decided I must have gone mad, so they tied me up and carried me back to the ship.

The captain, Pedro de Mendez, was a very good man. Although at first he didn't believe my story, he untied me once I'd promised not to try to escape.

We arrived in Lisbon. The good captain let me stay with him and even gave me a suit of his own clothes, which I wore after I'd let them air for a day, to get the smell of Yahoo out of them.

By the time a week had gone past I could look out of the window at humans without being too terrified. I still found them all revolting, though, and found it hard to believe that even the good captain wasn't going to attack me.

The captain put me on a ship going to England. I arrived on 5th December 1715, and by three o'clock in the afternoon I was home.

My family was full of joy at the sight of me – but I'm afraid it was hard for me to be very pleased to see them. To me, they all looked just like Yahoos.

I, Lemuel Gulliver, declare that this is the true story of my travels. I could easily have made things up, but I would never say *the thing that is not* because of my respect for my dear master Houyhnhnm. I haven't written this to make myself famous, but because I lived with the Houyhnhnms for a long time, so I know I have important things to tell people.

Some people have said I should tell the army and navy exactly where all the countries I visited can be found, so that they can be helped. But as I doubt the people I visited would accept help unless they were conquered, taken as slaves, or killed, I don't think I'll bother.

Now I am home, I am going to keep looking at myself in the mirror until I get used to being Yahoo-shaped. I hope I'll soon stop being afraid that everyone I see is going to rip me apart with their teeth and nails.

And in the meantime, I'm going to spend a lot of time in my stables, talking to my horses.

Jonathan Swift
(born 1667, died 1745)

Jonathan Swift was born in Dublin, Ireland. His father died before Swift was born and his mother, who was left without any money, was unable to support her family. For the first years of his life, Swift lived in England, until aged four he was sent back to Ireland to live with his uncle.

Aged 14, Swift went to study at Trinity College in Dublin. After his degree, he moved to England. He was to move back and forth to England and Ireland many times for work and personal reasons. Throughout his life Swift suffered from poor health. He had Ménière's Disease, which causes dizziness, nausea and hearing loss.

Swift became a priest in the Church of Ireland and was famous for his essay writing. He was friendly with many other well-known writers and wrote for several magazines. He was a founder of the Scribblers Club, which had several famous writers and poets among its members.

For nearly thirty years from 1713, Swift was Dean of St Patrick's Cathedral in Dublin. From 1738 his health began to worsen, and he suffered from memory loss. He once said to a poet when they were looking up at the withered crown of a tree, 'I shall be like that tree, I shall die from the top.'

Swift died in Dublin in 1745 and left behind a vast amount of poetry and prose, although with the exception of *Gulliver's Travels,* much of it is no longer read.

Best known works
Gulliver's Travels

Sally Prue

Sally Prue was born in 1958 (no one knows where). She was adopted when she was six months old and brought up in Hertfordshire in a house where no one read stories. She always wanted to be an explorer, but when she was a child nearly all her exploring had to be done between the covers of library books.

When she left school she went to work in the paper mill with the rest of her family. She started writing seriously when her younger daughter started nursery school, and filled in the years until her books began to be published teaching recorder and piano.

Sally still lives in Hertfordshire with her husband and elder daughter.

She says, 'I like books with adventures, funny bits, good characters and interesting ideas which give me things to think about. When I was young, *Gulliver's Travels* (in a short version, a bit like this one) was one of my favourites, so I was delighted to have the chance to re-read it and to tell the story again.

Gulliver's Travels sets out to make fun of human life. Even though the book was written in the 1720s, people are still very much as Lemuel Gulliver found them.

I believe that Jonathan Swift's masterpiece will continue to be wise and funny as long as there are people to enjoy it.'

Notes about this book

The main character in the book, Lemuel Gulliver, is a doctor and sea captain who tells of his travels to different places and the adventures he has there.

The book is made up of four parts. During the first voyage Gulliver is shipwrecked on the island of Lilliput, where the people are only six inches tall. Their vanity and self-importance seem all the more silly because of their tiny size. Gulliver escapes from Lilliput and returns to England, but soon sets out on his second voyage, which takes him to Brobdingnag, where he meets a race of giants as big compared to him as he is to the Lilliputians.

On the third voyage, Gulliver finds himself on the flying island of Laputa where the people are obsessed by science but their knowledge is useless because they know little or nothing of ordinary life. Gulliver then meets a race of people who never die, but who cannot enjoy this gift because they become senile in old age.

Finally, his fourth voyage takes him to a land where the horses are intelligent and polite, but the people, called the Yahoos, are dirty and inferior. He ends up admiring the horses, not the people.

Gulliver's Travels, as well as being entertaining, shows how humans behave foolishly or vainly, or try to gain power over others. Swift is saying that people should try to be humble and act decently toward one another.

Page 5

* **Tasmania** A large island off the south-east corner of the Australian mainland.

* **capsized** Turned upside down.

Pages 9–10
* **admiral** A person of a very senior rank in the navy.
* **'enough food for 1,728 of his people. I was twelve times taller, wider and deeper than a Lilliputian...'** Because Gulliver has a volume 1,728 times bigger than a Lilliputian (1,728 = 12 x 12 x 12), he needs 1,728 times as much food.

Page 13
* **treachery** To betray someone you are close to by breaking their trust. Gulliver is wrongly accused of betraying the Lilliputians.

Page 16
* **nardac** Swift made this up to mean a Lilliputian duke.

Page 19
* **king's council** A king's officials and advisers.

Page 20
* **greased it** Rubbed grease into the boat to make it waterproof.
* **linen** Cloth made from the plant called flax.

Page 23
* **Straits of Madagascar** The stretch of water between Africa and the island of Madagascar.

Page 24
* **scythe** A long curved blade with a wooden handle used for cutting grass or wheat.

Page 31
* **clockwork** The machinery that drives an old-fashioned watch or clock. It has many cogs and a spring.

* **stubble** Short bristly hairs that grow on a man's chin when he has not shaved for a few days.

Page 32
* **page** A boy who runs errands for the queen.

Page 39
* **parliament/Members of Parliament** A group of people elected to make a country's laws.

Page 40
* **plots and rebellions** A plot is a secret plan. A rebellion is an attempt to remove a leader and replace them.

Page 46
* **corn** Here, corn means an area of thick skin on a toe.

Page 49
* **eggheads** An egghead is a very clever person.

Page 50
* **46 North, Longitude 183** A way of describing an exact position on the face of the earth is to give the number of degrees north or south of the equator (latitude) and the number of degrees east or west of the Greenwich meridian (longitude). Gulliver's position is imaginary because the maximum number of degrees longitude in either direction is 180!

Page 55
* **famine** A severe shortage of food.

Page 68
* **imitating** Copying.